Welcome back

1 Höre dir das Lied an.

2 Lies die Aktivitäten und nummeriere die Bilder.

3 Was machen die Kinder? Sprich mit einem Partnerkind darüber.

8 

Activities at school:
1 counting
2 drawing
3 playing
4 reading
5 dancing
6 singing
7 writing
8 speaking
9 working with computers
10 learning about nature

1 

10 

4 Befrage die anderen Kinder.

Children of the world

1 Schau in deinem Textbook auf Seite 4 und 5 nach und fülle die Tabelle aus.

	name?	where from?	special information?
	John	Great Britain	His favourite football team is Chelsea.
		Ireland	Her favourite colour is ______
			Her favourite pet is her ______
			He likes playing ______
	Samuel		He is ______ years old.
			She has got ______ and ______

2 Sprich über die Kinder mit einem Partnerkind.

his → sein/e
her → ihr/e

Where is Maureen from?

What do you know about Maureen?

Maureen is from Ireland.

Her favourite colour is green.

More about Raj

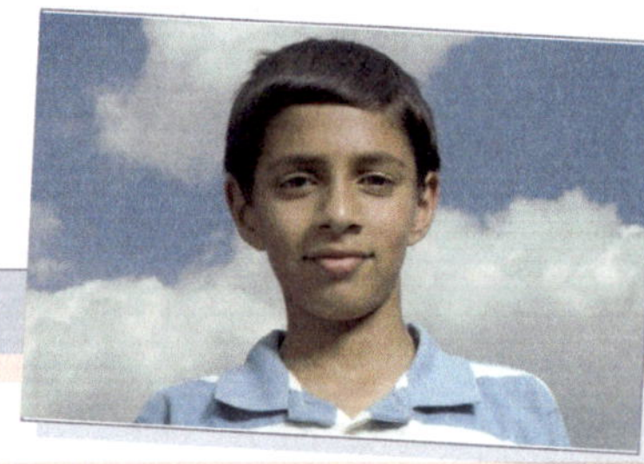

1 Höre dir den Text an und lies mit.

From: raj@email.co.in

To: ben@email.co.uk

Subject: Hello from Mumbai

Hi Ben,
My name is Raj and I'm 10 years old. I live in Mumbai, a big city in India.
My dad is a teacher and my mum is a vet. I go to an international school. That's great because we must speak English in the classroom. Dad says speaking English is good for getting a job. My favourite subjects are English and Maths. In the afternoon we often play cricket in the schoolyard. At the weekend I often go swimming with my father.
What about you? Would you like to be my pen pal?
Best regards, Raj

send

2 Was hast du verstanden?
Sprich darüber auf Deutsch.

Raj ist 10 Jahre alt.

Er geht zu einer ...

Sein Vater ist ...

...

3 Lies und beantworte die Fragen.

1	How old is Raj?	He is
2	Where does Raj live?	He lives
3	What is his mother's job?	His mother
4	What language does Raj speak at school?	He speaks
5	What are Raj's favourite subjects?	His favourite
6	What does Raj do at the weekend?	He often goes

Back at school

1 Löse das Kreuzworträtsel.

Across →

1 It's a new language for British children.
2 The children learn to read and write.
3 They can play ball games.
4 The children count and work with numbers.
5 They work with computers.
6 It's a meal for all the children.
7 It's a meeting of all the children at school.
8 The children plan and build things.

Down ↓

1 It's the last lesson on Friday.
2 They sing and play some instruments.
3 The children learn about nature.
4 It's fun to draw and paint.

~~German~~, Sport, ICT, school dinner, Assembly, Music, Art, English, Maths, Crafts, Science, Golden Time

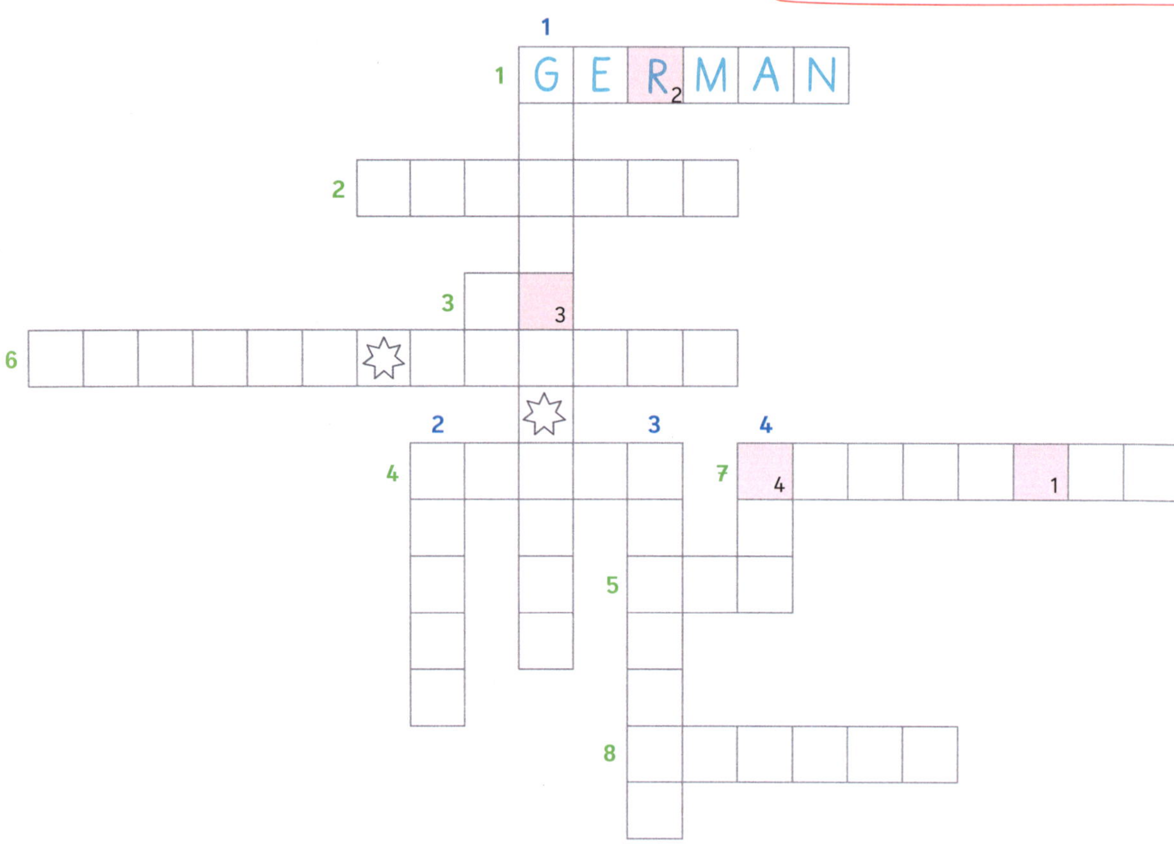

2 Schreibe das Lösungswort auf. Was mag Sara am liebsten?

I like many subjects at school,

but ___ ___ ___ ___ k is best.
1 2 3 4

LET'S PRACTISE!

Teachers and subjects

1 Schau dir die Bilder genau an. Was unterrichten die Lehrerinnen und Lehrer?

Schau nach auf Seite 6 und 7 in deinem TB.

Park school

Ms Nowdan

headmistress

Ms Philips

M______

Mr Baker

E______

Ms Li

M______

Ms Hall

S______

Mr Small

S______

Ms Dinsey

A______

Mr Müller

G______

Ms Brown

I______

2 Höre dir den Dialog an und lies mit.

3 Sprich über Lisas Lehrerinnen und Lehrer.

4 Sprich über deine Lehrerinnen und Lehrer.

What time ...?

1 Lies und verbinde.

10:15 | 10:30 | 11:00 | 10:00 | 10:45

It's ten o'clock. | It's ten fifteen. | It's ten thirty. | It's ten forty-five. | It's eleven o'clock.

2 Höre dir den Text auf CD an und nummeriere die Bilder.

3 Höre dir den Text noch einmal an und umkreise die richtige Uhrzeit.

☐ 

10:15 | 10:30

1 

08:00 | 08:45

☐ 

09:15 | 09:30

☐ 

11:45 | 12:45

4 Lies und beantworte die Fragen.

1. What time do you start from home? I start at ...

2. What time does your school begin? My school begins at...

Honey page – Back to school

1 Das sind meine wichtigsten Wörter zum Thema Stundenplan. Schreibe die Wörter in den Rahmen, die du dir merken möchtest.

Schau nach auf den Seiten 6–9 im TB!

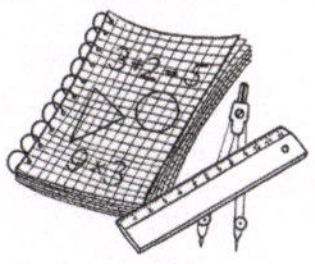

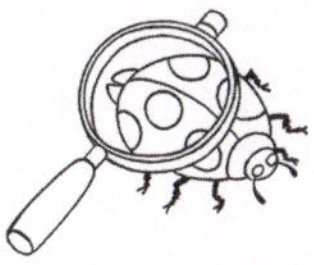
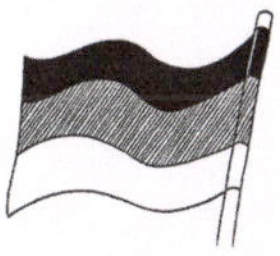
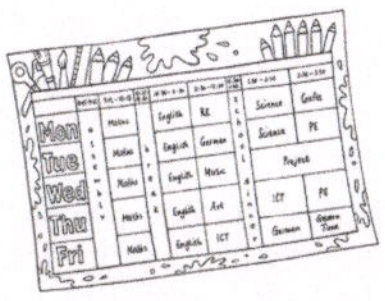
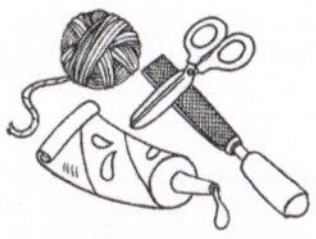

2 Ich kann meine Lieblingsfächer aufzählen.

My favourite subjects are ______________________

____

3 Ich kann bei einigen Fächern begründen, warum ich sie mag oder nicht mag.

I like ICT because I like working with computers.

I don't like Maths because I don't like counting.

German is on Monday at 9.15.

4 Ich kann sagen, wann ich einzelne Unterrichtsfächer habe.

Maths is on ______________ at ______________

PE is on ______________ at ______________

Science is on ______________ at ______________

My day

1 Finde die Wörter und löse das Rätsel. Schreibe auf.

2 Lies die Sätze.

	A	B	C	D
1	~~Lisa~~	at 8.30 a.m.	birthday party	~~Ben's~~
2	at 6.30 p.m.	~~meets~~	in the evening.	and
3	and	go to school	Cameron	brushes her teeth.
4	watch TV	~~Ravi~~	~~at 4 o'clock.~~	In the morning
5	washes her face.	~~Lisa~~	~~Lisa~~	and
6	at 7 o'clock.	starts	~~Grandpa~~	~~her friends~~

	A1	B2	D6	C4
1	Lisa	meets	her friends	at 4 o'clock.

	D1	C1	B6	A2
2	Ben's			

	C5	A3	C6	A4	C2
3	Lisa		Grandpa		

	B4	D2	C3	B3	B1
4	Ravi				

	D4	B5	D5
5		Lisa	

3 Finde das passende Bild zu den Sätzen aus Aufgabe 1.

☐

☐

1

☐

☐

LET'S PRACTISE!

My day

1 Lies.

get up | go to school | meet my friends | have lunch

have dinner | do my homework | watch TV

brush my teeth | put on my pyjamas

take a shower | go to school | have dinner

get dressed | wash my face

2 Schreibe über deinen Tag. Nutze die Wörter aus dem Kasten.

in the morning	in the afternoon	in the evening
I wash my face.	I meet my friends.	I watch TV.

3 Befragt euch gegenseitig über euren Tag.

Emma and Ben's morning

1 Höre dir den Text an und verbinde die Bilder mit der richtigen Uhrzeit.

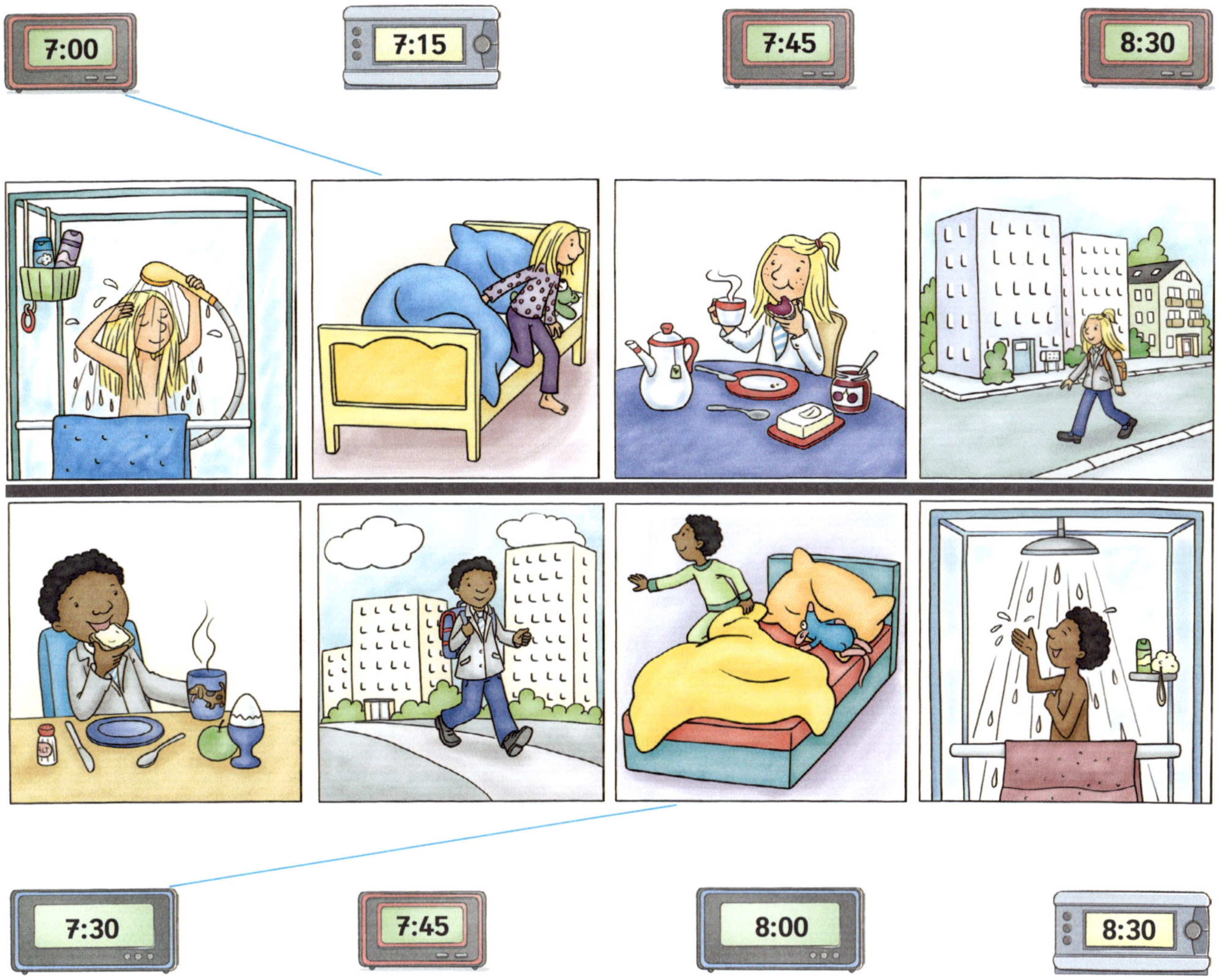

she gets
she has
she takes
she goes

2 Schreibe über Emmas Tag.

Emma gets up at ____________

____________ has breakfast at ____________

____________ takes a shower at ____________

____________ goes to school at ____________

Liam's day

1 Lies die E-Mail. Um was geht es?

2 Suche die Schlüsselwörter im Text.

3 Vergleiche mit einem Partnerkind.

From: liam@email.com

To: ben@email.co.uk

Subject: Hello from Atlanta

Hello Ben!
My name is Liam. I'm 10 years old. I'm from Atlanta, USA.
Every morning at 8.30 I go to school by school bus.
School starts at 9 o'clock.
My favourite subjects are English and ICT.
I have lunch at school.
In the afternoon I like to play the guitar. I play in our school band.
I also like to play American football.
I often do my homework in the school library.
At 4.30 I come home. Then I play with my friends.
I go to bed at 9 o'clock. I like to read in bed.
Best wishes, Liam

send

4 Lies und beantworte die Fragen.

9, ICT, 10, Atlanta, 9, 4.30

How old is Liam? – He is ________ years old.

Where is Liam from? – He is from ____________________, USA.

What time does school start? – School starts at ________ o'clock.

What are Liam's favourite subjects? – His favourite subjects are English and ____________.

When does he come home? – He comes home at __________.

What time does Liam go to bed? – He goes to bed at ________ o'clock.

This is my day

1 Schreibe über deinen Tag.

2 Stelle dein Ergebnis der Klasse vor.

I go to school – I wash my face – I get dressed – I get up –

I get up at

I have breakfast at

I go to school at

I do my homework at

I watch TV at

I go to bed at

– I watch TV – I have dinner– I go to bed – I put on my pyjamas –

I brush my teeth – I meet my friends – I have breakfast – I do my homework –

I have lunch – I take a shower – I take off my clothes

Honey page – My day

1 Das sind meine wichtigsten Wörter zum Thema My day.
Schreibe die Wörter in den Rahmen, die du dir merken möchtest.

Schau nach auf den Seiten 13 und 14 im TB!

2 Ich kann Ereignisse im Tagesablauf der Tageszeit zuordnen.

1. In the morning ...

2. In the afternoon ...

3. In the evening ...

☐	... I brush my teeth.	☐	... I watch TV.
1	... I get up.	☐	... I take a shower.
☐	... I do my homework.	☐	... I have breakfast.
☐	... I meet my friends.	☐	... I wash my face.
☐	... I have dinner.	☐	... I go to school.

3 Ich kann über meinen Tagesablauf sprechen.

What do you do in the morning?

In the morning, I ...

4 Ich kann diese Uhrzeiten benennen.

5 Ich kann andere Kinder zu ihrem Tagesablauf befragen und Fragen zu meinem Tagesablauf beantworten.

When do you ...?

I ... at ...

Our little town

1 Höre dir die CD an und nummeriere die Bilder.

2 Beschrifte die Puzzleteile.

Schau nach auf Seite 18 in deinem TB.

p

f

p

m

c

p

c

g

t

3 Finde das Lösungswort. Nutze die Buchstaben in den Puzzleteilen.

1	2	3	4	5	6	7	8	9
A								R

CD 30
Fö/Fo 15

LET'S PRACTISE! Our litte town

1 Höre dir die Wegbeschreibung an.

2 Höre dir die Wegbeschreibung noch einmal an und zeichne den Weg ein.

3 Übe den Dialog ein und spiele die Szene der Klasse vor.

turn left

turn right

cross, go straight on

Places in our town

1 Lies die Wörter und nummeriere die passenden Bilder.

1. town hall
2. playground
3. post office
4. cinema
5. hospital
6. St. Mary's Church
7. farmer's market
8. police station

☐ 

☐ 

1 

☐ 

2 

6 

☐ 

☐ 

2 Höre dir den Text von der CD an und lies mit.

3 Lies die Sätze und finde den beschriebenen Ort. Nummeriere.

6 This building is from 1450. Ninety steps lead up to the bell tower.

☐ It has seats for fifty people and shows films only on Saturday and Sunday.

☐ It has forty beds and a new cafeteria for patients, doctors and nurses.

☐ Ten police officers and two police dogs work in this building.

☐ It is a place where you can post your letters, postcards and parcels.

1 It is one of the oldest buildings in town. In the cellar you can visit the old prison.

2 Children love it. For the young kids we have swings and a slide, the older kids like the skaters' half pipe.

☐ On Saturdays, people buy fresh products from local farmers here. They like to listen to our local bagpiper, playing some Scottish tunes.

How to get to the ...

1 Lies den Text und unterstreiche die Schlüsselwörter.

2 Zeichne den Weg ein.

1. You are at the church.
Use the zebra crossing to cross the street.
Turn left and walk along Church Street.
Turn right into Park Road.
Walk straight on.
Which building is at the end of the road?

3 Wie kommst du zur Schule? Schreibe die Wegbeschreibung.

You start at the church.

Turn ______ and walk along Church Street. Turn ______ into

Rose Street. Turn ______ into Old Street.

The building you are looking for is on the ______.

My favourite place

1 Was kannst du über deinen Lieblingsplatz in deiner Stadt sagen? Lies und umkreise alle Orte blau und alle Adjektive rot.

shopping centre   big   park   old   sports centre

half pipe   football park

cinema   nice   beautiful

market   playground   new

swimming pool   small

cool   church   interesting

museum   super   modern   horse farm

2 Welcher Ort wird hier beschrieben? Verbinde den Text mit dem passenden Bild.

My favourite place is the park.
The park is old and very nice.
There is a new playground with a half pipe.
I love jogging and skating there.
It's cool!

3 Schreibe einen Text über deinen Lieblingsort.

swimming, playing, taking photos, going shopping, meeting friends, having a meal,

looking at, visiting,

My favourite place is ________________.

The ________ is ________ and ________.

There are ________________.

I love ________________

________________ there.

watching, going for a walk,

skating, running, jogging, relaxing, riding, buying, climbing, training, having a picnic

Honey page – Our little town

1 Das sind meine wichtigsten Wörter zum Thema Kleinstadt.
Schreibe die Wörter in den Rahmen, die du dir merken möchtest.

Schau nach auf Seite 19 im TB!

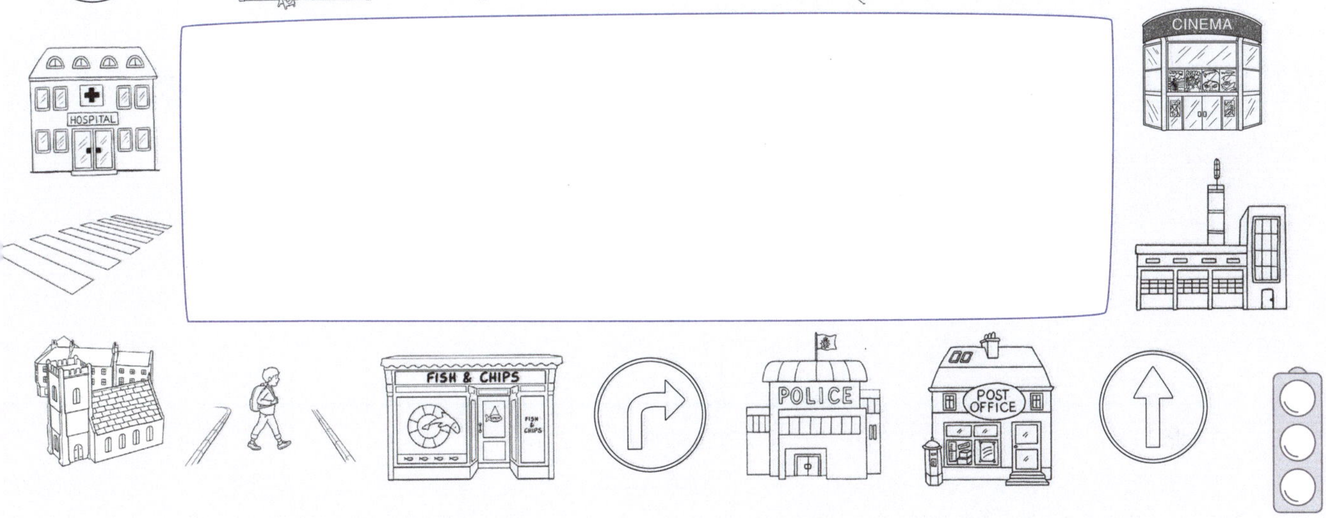

2 Ich kann die Sehenswürdigkeiten an meinem Ort aufzählen.

In my town you can visit ______

______

______

______

3 Ich kann nach dem Weg fragen und die Wegbeschreibung verstehen.

Schau dir die Karte auf Seite 17 an.

How do I get to the ______ ?

Turn ______

When I grow up

1 Suche die Berufe und kreise sie ein. (3→ / 5↓)

C	I	Y	W	F	R	S	F	H	R	Y	S	N	T
N	E	N	G	I	N	E	E	R	J	R	X	C	D
G	F	O	W	R	H	C	Z	D	I	W	T	B	S
A	S	B	R	E	A	O	N	O	X	A	G	U	U
R	T	O	U	F	I	M	H	K	F	I	H	I	C
D	Q	E	D	I	R	M	L	O	V	T	B	L	Z
E	N	G	B	G	D	W	D	A	I	R	H	D	J
N	X	M	M	H	R	D	R	H	F	E	B	E	L
E	A	C	S	T	E	N	G	M	J	S	G	R	B
R	R	R	Z	E	S	G	N	U	R	S	E	W	S
K	F	G	K	R	S	S	F	W	L	T	A	Y	P
P	O	L	I	C	E	☆	O	F	F	I	C	E	R
S	W	A	T	G	R	W	B	E	Z	H	U	J	P

2 Schau dir das Bild genau an. Welche Kleidung passt zu welchem Beruf? Beschrifte.

nurse | builder | police officer | firefighter | hairdresser | gardener

Daily jobs

1 Lies die Sätze und ergänze die fehlenden Wörter.

~~works~~	controls	cuts	puts out	repairs	constructs
plants	builds	sells	helps	looks	checks

I work
she works
he works

He works ____________ in a restaurant. He is a waiter.

She c ____________ the traffic. She is a police officer.

He p ____________ the fire. He is a firefighter.

He r ____________ cars. He is a car mechanic.

She h ____________ ill animals. She is a vet.

She c ____________ bridges. She is an engineer.

She p ____________ trees and bushes. She is a gardener.

He c ____________ hair. He is a hairdresser.

She s ____________ things. She is a shop assistant.

He b ____________ houses. He is a builder.

She l ____________ after animals. She is a zookeeper.

He ch ____________ your teeth. He is a dentist.

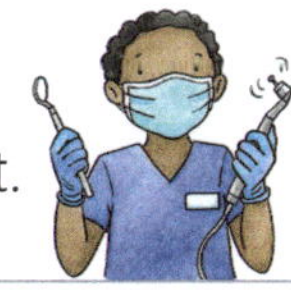

LET'S PRACTISE!

Where do they work and why?

1 Lies die Sätze.

2 Übe mit einem Partnerkind die Sätze.

A	nurse works in a hospital		because he / she likes to work with children.
	farmer works on a farm		because he / she likes to put out fires.
	shop assistant works in a clothes shop		because he / she wants to help ill people.
	zookeeper works in a zoo		because he / she likes fashion.
	firefighter works in a fire station		because he / she likes to work with animals.
	teacher works at school		because he / she likes animals.

3 Schreibe 2 Sätze auf.

A nurse works in a hospital because he wants to help ill people.

Mum's busy day

1 Schau dir die Bilder an.

1

2

3

4

5

6

2 Lies die Sätze und nummeriere.

- [ ] At lunchtime Mum often buys a sandwich and a cup of coffee at the snack bar.
- [1] Every morning at 8 o'clock my mum leaves the house to go to work.
- [ ] She waits at the bus stop and always takes the bus to the shopping centre at 8.20.
- [ ] We all have a nice meal in the evening and talk about our day.
- [ ] Mum has a nice little fashion shop next to the book shop. She sells T-shirts, dresses, jackets, skirts and pullovers.
- [ ] In the afternoon there are many ladies in her shop who want to buy something nice.

An emergency call

1 Höre dir das Telefongespräch an.

2 Lies dir die Sätze durch und verbinde die Fragen mit den richtigen Antworten.

3 Übe den Dialog und spiele die Szene der Klasse vor.

Emergency call: 999. How can I help you?	Peter Douglas
What is your name?	There is a fire in our kitchen.
Where do you live?	I live at 28 Lincoln Street.
Stay on the phone! Help is on the way!	Thank you!

5 Wann wählst du den Notruf? Kreuze an.

	😊	☹
Your pet is ill.		X
There is a fire in the house.		
There is a car accident.		
You lost your key.		
Your grandma falls and is not waking up.		

Notrufnummern

112

Germany

999

Great Britain

911

USA

CD 46
Fö/Fo 23

Honey page – When I grow up

1 Das sind meine wichtigsten Wörter zum Thema Berufe.
Schreibe die Wörter in den Rahmen, die du dir merken möchtest.

Schau nach auf Seite 25 im TB!

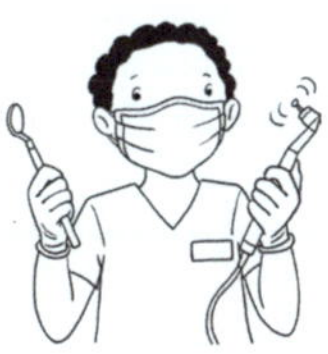   

2 Ich kann sagen, wer hier arbeitet.

A ______________________ works in a fire station.

A ______________________ works in a hospital.

A ______________________ works in a school.

A ______________________ works on a farm.

3 Ich kann begründen, warum diese Menschen ihren Beruf mögen.

A zookeeper works in a zoo ...

... because he/she likes animals.

A shop assistant ______________________

____

____

Animals

1 Schau dir die Fotos an. Welche Tiere erkennst du? Schreibe auf.

penguinhorseparrotpolar*beargoathippokangaroochimpanzee

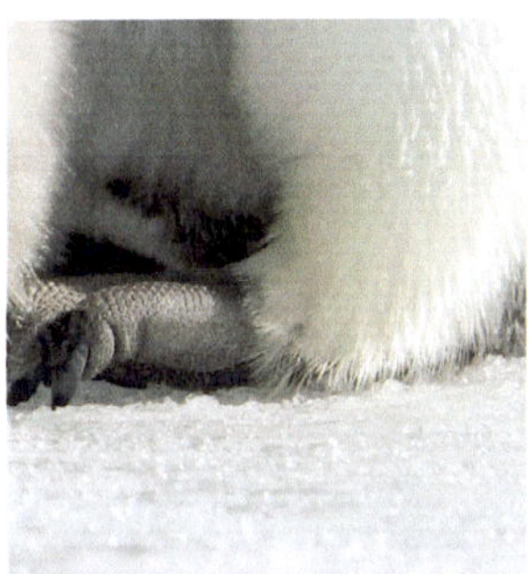

2 Ordne die Tiere den Verben zu. Ergänze die Tabelle.

Schau nach auf Seite 33 im TB!

 jump	 climb	 dive	 run	 fly	 swim	 lay eggs
kangaroo	chimpanzee	duck	tiger	parrot	duck	penguin

LET'S PRACTISE!

Guess my animal

1 Höre dir die Wörter an und zeige auf die Körperteile.

2 Höre dir den Dialog an und lies mit.

3 Übe den Dialog.

4 Suche dir ein Tier für das Ratespiel aus.
Vervollständige die Tabelle und spiele das Ratespiel.

animal	size	body parts	activities
elephant	big	trunk	run
	long	neck	

Farm animal quiz

1 Beantworte die Fragen und finde den richtigen Weg.

Schau in einem Wörterbuch nach!

Where do pigs live?

Pigs live on a farm.

Pigs live in a flat.

Chickens lay five eggs a day.

Sorry, that's wrong.

Yes, I think so.

No, they only lay one or two eggs a day.

What do you call baby pigs?

piglets

lambs

Chickens live up to 20 years.

Oh, no.

No, chickens live up to 7 years.

Yes, they live up to 20 years.

Which bird is bigger? Turkey or chicken?

That's's wrong. Look it up on page 34 in your textbook.

chicken

turkey

No ☹.

Goats can fly.

Yes, they can.

Oh, oh, oh!

No, they can't.

Do cows have humps?

No, they don't.

Yes, they do.

Well done!

Try again.

Chimpanzees: Endangered animals

1 Lies dir den Text durch.

2 Beantworte die Fragen.

3 Vergleiche mit einem Partnerkind.

Charlie is a chimpanzee. Chimpanzees are big apes.
They are not monkeys because they do not have a tail.
They are shy animals and live in the jungle.
Chimpanzees live in big groups of 30–80 animals.
They are noisy and intelligent.
The strongest chimpanzee is the boss of the group.
He protects the mothers and their babies.
Chimpanzees sleep in tree nests.

What are chimpanzees?	Chimpanzees are ______________
Where do chimpanzees live?	They live in ______________
Do chimpanzees live alone or in groups?	They live ______________
Where do chimpanzees sleep?	They sleep ______________

4 Kennst du andere bedrohte Tierarten?

A trip to the zoo

1. Höre dir die Dialoge an.
2. Finde die richtige Reihenfolge. Nummeriere.
3. Übe einen Dialog ein. Spiele ihn der Klasse vor.

Thank you. [ ]

You're welcome. [6]

It's 13 pounds. [ ]

How much is 1 ticket? [1]

Here you are. That's 39 pounds. [ ]

I'd like to buy 3 tickets. [ ]

What do polar bears eat? [3]

I like the polar bears best. [ ]

They come from the Arctic. [ ]

Which animals do you like best? [1]

They eat fish and meat. [ ]

Where do they come from? [5]

CD 54
Fö/Fo 28

Honey page – Animals

1 Das sind meine wichtigsten Wörter zum Thema Tiere.
Schreibe die Wörter in den Rahmen, die du dir merken möchtest.

 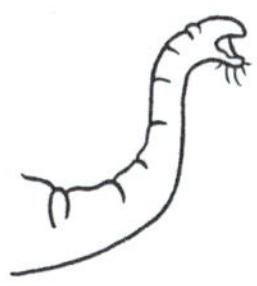   

2a Ich kann Fragen über ein Tier stellen und beantworten.

1. Where do chimpanzees live?	☐ Chimpanzees eat fruits, plants and meat.
2. What do chimpanzees eat?	☐ They live up to 40 years.
3. How long do chimpanzees live?	☐ Chimpanzees live in the jungle.

2b Ich kann ein Tierratespiel spielen.

What colour is it?

Is it big or small?

Can it ...?

Has it got ...?

3 Das hat mir beim Lesen der Sachtexte geholfen.

- ○ Ich höre mir den Lesetext an.
- ○ Ich suche nach bekannten Wörtern.
- ○ Ich achte auf helfende Bilder.
- ○ Ich achte auf die Überschrift.
- ○ Ich versuche mir den Inhalt zu erschließen, auch wenn ich nicht alle Wörter verstehe.
- ○ Ich schlage unbekannte Wörter nach.

Earth Day

1 Spiele das Würfelspiel. Erkläre die Bilder, wenn du auf das entsprechende Spielfeld kommst.

LET'S PRACTISE! Helping nature

1 Höre dir den Dialog an.

2 Übe den Dialog.

batteries

broken glass

Where does the broken glass go?

The broken glass goes into the glass bag.

wrappings

empty bottles

Where do the wrappings go?

The wrappings go into the plastic bag.

newspapers

comics

old shoe

cans

3 Vervollständige die Sätze.

The batteries go into the battery box.

The comics go into the ______.

The cans go into the ______.

The ______ go into the ______.

In a family

1 Höre dir die Sätze an. Nummeriere.

☐ ☐ ☐ 1

☐ ☐ ☐ ☐

2 Lies die Sätze und finde das passende Bild. Nummeriere.

3 Überprüfe deine Antworten mit einem Partnerkind.

4 Wer handelt umweltbewusst? Umkreise die Personen.

The woman leaves the heating on.	1
The boy takes a bath.	
The man brushes his teeth. The water is running.	
The girl rides her bike.	
Grandpa switches the light off.	
The girl leaves the fridge door open.	
The boy throws food into the bin.	
The woman puts the newspaper into the paper bin.	

How green are you?

1 Beantworte die Fragen.

www.areyougreen.co.uk

	Are you green? Test yourself.		points
	Do you switch off the light / computer / TV ...?	Always Sometimes Never	3 2 1
	Do you recycle your rubbish? (glass, plastic, cans, paper)	Always Sometimes Never	3 2 1
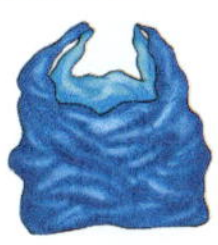	Do you use plastic bags for shopping?	Always Sometimes Never	1 2 3
	Do you walk to school, take public transport or go by bike?	Always Sometimes Never	3 2 1
	Do you throw away any food?	Always Sometimes Never	1 2 3
	Do you buy things at second hand shops?	Always Sometimes Never	3 2 1

2 Addiere die Punkte.
Wie umweltbewusst bist du?

Your points: ____________

14–18 points
Well done! You are very green!

12 / 11 points
Okay! You can do more!

6–10 points
Please do more for our planet!!!

3 Sprich über deine Ergebnisse.

I always switch off the light in my room.

I never throw any food away.

Upcycling

Do you need a birthday present for a friend? What about upcycling an old can to make a simple but stylish pencil holder? It is for pencils, markers, paint brushes and more.

This is what you need:

a clean can

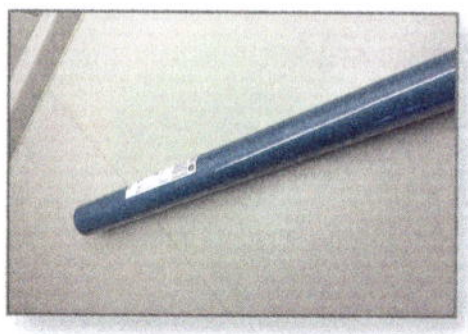
coloured paper

a set of eyeballs

a marker

a glue stick

some tape

1 Lies die Erklärung. Finde die richtige Reihenfolge und nummeriere die Sätze.

- [6] Draw a smiley face on your pencil holder. Then your pencil holder is finished.
- [ ] Then wrap the paper around the can.
- [ ] Stick the two eyeballs on the can.
- [ ] Fix the paper with a piece of tape.
- [1] Cut your paper to fit the can.
- [ ] Now fasten the paper with the glue stick.

1

2

3
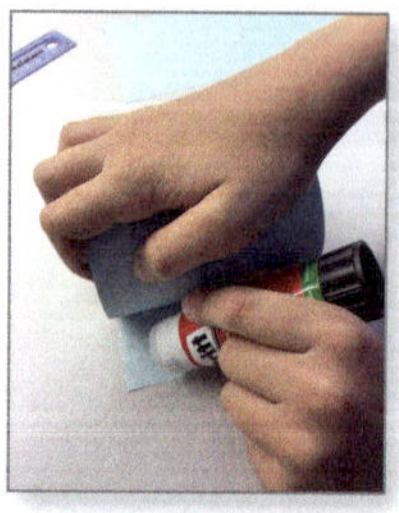

4

5

6

2 Bastele deinen eigenen Bleistifthalter.

3 Suche im Internet nach weiteren Ideen, wie du deine alten Sachen upcyceln kannst.

Honey page – Earth Day

1 Das sind meine wichtigsten Wörter zum Thema Earth Day.
Schreibe die Wörter in den Rahmen, die du dir merken möchtest.

Schau nach auf Seite 39 im TB!

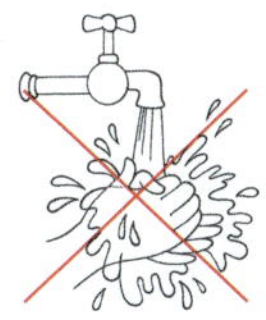

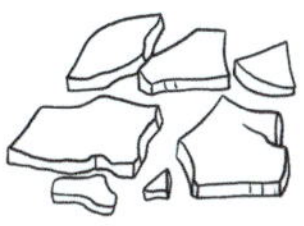

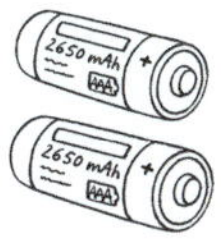

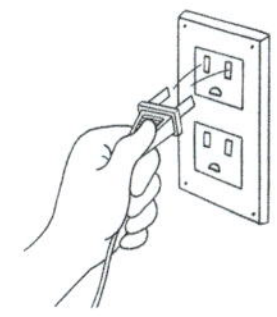

2 Ich kann aufschreiben, was man tun kann, um die Umwelt zu schonen.

I can save water.

3 Ich kann sagen, wie ich Müll richtig entsorgen kann.

Where does broken glass go?

Broken glass goes into ...

Where do comics go?

Comics go into ...

Holidays

1 Beschrifte die Dinge im Bild.

2 Markiere die drei Wörter, die nicht im Bild vorkommen.

3 Vervollständige die Sätze. Die markierten Wörter helfen dir.

flippers	spade	picnic basket	volleyball	sunglasses
fishing net	air mattress	~~seagull~~	books	snorkel
boat	sun cream	sandcastle	lifeguard	sun hat

1. A seagull is a grey and white bird that lives at the sea.

2. If you are in danger, the l__________ can save you.

3. Children love building a s__________ on the beach.

FC/WC 208–212

LET'S PRACTISE!

Holiday plans

1. Höre dir den Dialog an.
2. Vervollständige die Sätze.
3. Höre dir die Sätze noch einmal an und überprüfe.
4. Übe die Dialoge.

a barbecue | stand-up paddling | in the sun | fishing

5. Male und schreibe über das, was du gerne machen würdest.

What are you going to do?

I'm going to ________________

____

Ben in danger

1 Höre dir den Text an und lies mit.

2 Hast du die Geschichte verstanden?
Sprich mit einem Partnerkind.

3 Beantworte die Fragen auf Deutsch.

It is a nice summer day **at the beach**.

But there are some **dark clouds** in the sky.

Ben swims on his air mattress **in the sea**.

He forgets about the **warning flag**.

Suddenly the dark clouds move in and **a strong wind comes up**.

Ben's dog Fred watches Ben on his air mattress from the beach.

He feels that **Ben is in danger**.

The wind gets so strong that **Ben can't get back to the beach**.

Fred runs to the lifeguard tower and barks loudly.

The **lifeguards** look for Ben from the tower.

They can see that he is in danger.

The lifeguards quickly jump into their boat to **rescue Ben**.

Soon **Ben is** safely **back on the beach**.

His family is very glad and Fred is happy, too.

In future Ben will always **watch out for the flags**

before he goes into the water.

Wie war das Wetter?
Warum konnte Ben nicht zurückkommen?
Wer informierte die Lifeguards?
Wie wird Ben gerettet?

CD 74
KV 76

Stay safe

1 Schau dir die Schilder an.

2 Lies die Sätze.

3 Verbinde.

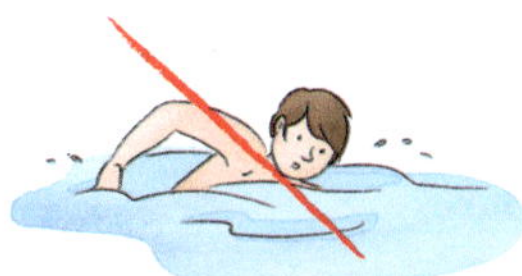

At this beach there are lifeguards.

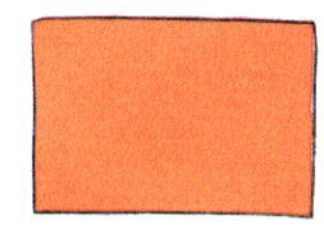

Danger! No swimming!

Do not swim here.

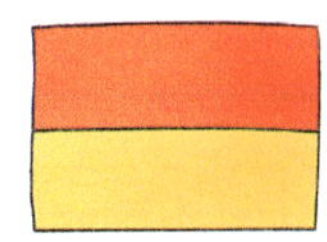

Lifeguard on duty.

Today you can swim here.

Caution! Seek advice.

Ask the lifeguards if you can swim today.

Safe to swim.

Be careful, this area is for surfing only.

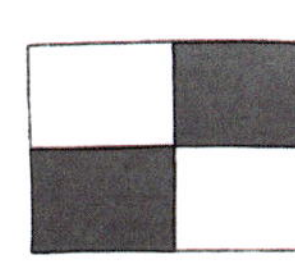

Surfing area. No swimming.

4 Male ein Schild für die Warnung.

Sharks in the water.
It is dangerous to swim here!

Your holiday plans

1 Höre dir die Wörter an und lies mit.

2 Wähle Wörter für deinen Urlaubswunsch aus und mache dir Notizen.

3 Sprich über deine Pläne.

beach

forest

mountains

lake

river

city
______ ______ ______

go swimming

go hiking

go climbing

go sightseeing

go biking

go fishing

visit

take a photo
______ ______ ______

My family and I are going to go to ...

______

______

______

I am going to ...

______

______

and ...

______

4 Lies Tims E-Mail. Sie kann dir bei deinem Text helfen.

Hi, Peter!
My grandparents and I are going to go to a lake in the mountains in Italy. We are going to go hiking and do some mountain biking.
From, Tim

TARGET TASK

5 Write about your holiday plans.

FC/WC 201–207, 213–214
CD 77

Honey page – Holidays

1 Das sind meine wichtigsten Wörter zum Thema Ferien.
Schreibe die Wörter in den Rahmen, die du dir merken möchtest.

Schau nach auf den Seiten 47 und 48 im TB!

  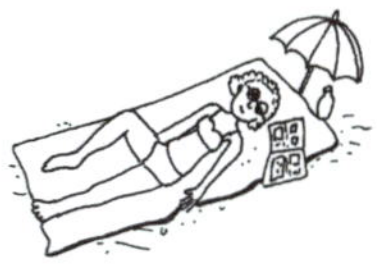 

2 Ich kann sagen, wohin ich in die Ferien fahren werde, mit wem und was ich dort machen werde.

Schau nach auf Seite 41 im WB!

I am going to go ______________________

____

____

____

____

3 Das hat mir beim Lesen der Bildergeschichte geholfen.

- ◯ Ich höre mir den Lesetext an.
- ◯ Ich suche nach bekannten Wörtern.
- ◯ Ich achte auf helfende Bilder.
- ◯ Ich achte auf die Überschrift.
- ◯ Ich versuche mir den Inhalt zu erschließen, auch wenn ich nicht alle Wörter verstehe.
- ◯ Ich schlage unbekannte Wörter nach.

Thanksgiving

1 Lies dir die Sätze durch und nummeriere die richtigen Bilder.

2 Löse das Kreuzworträtsel. Schreibe im Crossword mit Großbuchstaben.

3 Vergleiche mit einem Partnerkind.

~~fish~~ November dinner pilgrims Mayflower football parade turkey

Across →

The **1** came to America.

On Thanksgiving people watch **2** on TV.

Thanksgiving is on the fourth Thursday in **3** .

Many families have a **4** for Thanksgiving dinner.

Down ↓

The pilgrims learned to catch **5** .

The name of the ship was **6** .

In big cities there is a **7** .

People eat turkey for **8** .

5 F I S H

1 P I . . . . M .

6 M

7 P

2 F

8 D

3 N

4 T

1

Fo/Fo 38

Leprechaun quiz

1 Lies die Geschichte im Textbook auf den Seiten 56 und 57.

2 Lies die Sätze und kreise die richtige Lösung ein.

1. One day a young man walked through ...
... a forest in England. **D**
... a forest in Ireland. **S**

2. The man heard ...
... the tap-tapping of a shoe. **A**
... the tap-tapping of a hammer. **H**

3. The leprechaun was ...
... reading a golden book. **O**
... repairing a shoe. **A**

4. Leprechauns have got ...
... a pot of soup. **N**
... a pot of gold. **M**

5. The man asked the leprechaun ...
... "Where is your money?" **H**
... "Where is your pot of gold?" **R**

6. The man wanted the leprechaun's gold and marked the bush ...
... with a red shoe. **S**
... with a red scarf. **O**

7. The man ran away ...
... to get the gold. **T**
... to get a spade. **C**

8. Left behind in the forest, the leprechaun played a trick on him and ...
... put his gold under the bush. **D**
... put a red scarf on every bush. **K**

This is a symbol of Ireland:

___ ___ ___ ___ ___ ___ ___ ___
1 2 3 4 5 6 7 8

Alphabet

1 Höre dir den Text an und lies mit.

a apple

b boat

c cat

d dog

e egg

f fish

g girl

h hamster

i ice cream

j jam

k king

l lamp

m mouse

n nose

o orange

p pencil

q queen

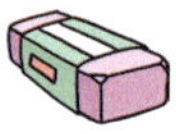
r rubber

s snake

t toilet

u uniform

v vampire

w witch

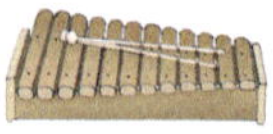
x xylophone

y yo-yo

z zebra

2 Welcher Buchstabe ist dein Lieblingsbuchstabe?

3 Höre dir das Lied zum Alphabet an. Sing mit.

4 Schreibe deinen Namen auf und übe ihn zu buchstabieren.

Can you spell your name?

My name is Ben.
B – E - N

Write your name: ____________________

Aus rechtlichen Gründen kann das Lied zum Alphabet nicht per QR-Code angeboten werden.

CD 83-85
KV 87-88
Fö/Fo 40

Number plates

1 Höre dir den Text über Autokennzeichen an und verbinde die Fahrzeuge mit den richtigen Nummernschildern.

YR53 JEP

PM59 RMW

TA11 BFE

CM10 BLE

2 Übe das Buchstabieren der Nummernschilder.

3 Schau dir die letzten 3 Buchstaben an. Findest du die versteckten Tiernamen?

BG02 ABT	HX55 GIP	HC56 ATC
1 bat	2 p	3 c
EL05 DGO	NP10 TRA	CM60 WCO
4 d	5 r	6 c

4 Erfinde eigene Nummernschilder. Nutze die Wörter im Wörterkasten und erfinde eigene Rätsel.

toy   leg   fun   day   arm   bell   hat   day

MS80 YTO		
1 toy	2	3

Fit for 5!

1 Lies die Fragen und nummeriere die deutsche Übersetzung.

2 Übe Dialoge ein.

Alles über mich ...

1. Wie heißt du?
2. Wie alt bist du?
3. Wie geht es dir?
4. Wo kommst du her?
5. Wie lautet deine Telefonnummer?
6. Hast du eine Schwester oder einen Bruder?
7. Was ist dein Lieblings-Hobby?
8. Hast du ein Haustier?
9. Was möchtest du werden, wenn du erwachsen bist?

☐	Have you got a sister or a brother?
☐	How are you?
☐	What's your phone number?
☐	How old are you?
☐	Where are you from?
9	What do you want to be when you grow up?
1	What's your name?
☐	What's your favourite hobby?
☐	Have you got a pet?

In der Schule ...

10. Wo ist dein Radiergummi?
11. Hast du einen Füller?
12. Darf ich bitte dein Lineal haben?
13. Welche Farbe hat dein Etui?
14. Wann haben wir Englisch?
15. Magst du Sport?
16. Was ist dein Lieblingsfach?
17. Was hast du in deiner Brotdose?

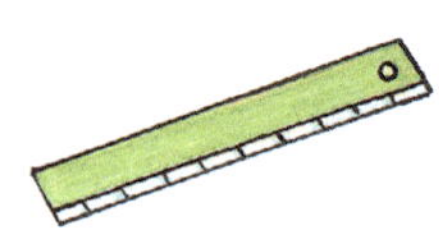

☐	Do you like PE?
☐	Can I have your ruler, please?
☐	Have you got a pen?
☐	Where is your rubber?
17	What have you got in your lunchbox?
14	When do we have English?
☐	What colour is your pencil case?
☐	What's your favourite subject?

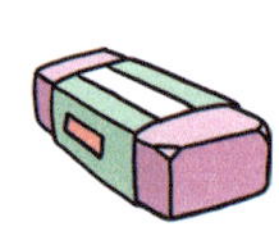

Fit for 5!

Beim Einkauf ...

18. Kann ich dir helfen?
19. Ich hätte gerne ein neues T-shirt.
20. Wie teuer ist das?
21. Das kostet 15 Pfund.
22. Danke!
23. Bitte!

- [ ] Thank you.
- [ ] Can I help you?
- [ ] That's 15 pounds.
- [19] I'd like a new T-shirt.
- [ ] Here you are.
- [ ] How much is it?

In der Stadt ...

24. Was möchtest du gerne machen?
25. Lass uns ins Kino gehen!
26. Wie kommen wir dort hin?
27. Lass uns den Bus nehmen!
28. Können Sie mir bitte helfen?
29. Entschuldigen Sie bitte. Wo ist der Spielplatz?
30. Wie spät ist es?
31. Wie ist das Wetter?

- [26] How do we get there?
- [ ] Excuse me. Where is the playground?
- [ ] What time is it?
- [ ] What would you like to do?
- [ ] What's the weather like?
- [ ] Let's take the bus.
- [ ] Can you help me, please?
- [25] Let's go to the cinema.

Alles über Tiere ...

32. Was ist dein Lieblingstier?
33. Welche Farbe hat es?
34. Ist es groß oder klein?
35. Kann es fliegen?
36. Hat es zwei Beine?

- [ ] Is it big or small?
- [35] Can it fly?
- [ ] Has it got two legs?
- [ ] What colour is it?
- [ ] What's your favourite animal?

An important phone call

1 Schau dir das Bild an.
Um was geht es in diesem Telefongespräch?

2 Höre dir das Telefongespräch noch einmal an. Beantworte die Fragen.

1. Lisa gets a phone call from Amber. Who is she?
   ◯ Lisa's new teacher. ◯ Lisa's mentor.

2. How old is Lisa's mentor, Amber?
   ◯ She is twelve (12). ◯ She is fourteen (14).

3. What are Lisa's favourite subjects?
   ◯ She likes Maths and PE. ◯ She likes Maths and German.

4. Will Lisa have new subjects at London Park School?
   ◯ No, she will not have new subjects.
   ◯ Yes, she will have History and Geography.

5. How will Lisa get to school?
   ◯ She will walk. ◯ She will take the bus.

6. Will Lisa wear a school uniform at London Park School?
   ◯ Yes, she will wear a dark red and grey school uniform.
   ◯ Yes, she will wear a black and white school uniform.

7. Will Lisa have some afternoon activities?
   ◯ Yes, she will. ◯ No, she will not.

CD 89

LET'S PRACTISE!

Find someone who ...

1 Höre dir den Dialog an.

2 Welche Fragen musst du stellen?

3 Frage deine Mitschülerinnen und Mitschüler.

Do you like ...?
Yes, I do. / No, I don't.
Will you ...?
Yes, I will. / No, I won't.

Do you like Maths?

Will you take the bus to school?

No, I don't like Maths.

Yes, I will take the bus.

Find someone who ...	This is what you ask:	Name
likes German.	Do you like German?	
doesn't like PE.		
will have new subjects at school.	Will you have new subjects at school?	
will have History at school.	Will you	
will take the bus to school.	Will you	
will walk to school.	Will you	
will do sport in the afternoon.	Will you	
will play an instrument in the afternoon.	Will you	

CD 90

Learn more ...

Rhyme words

1 Was reimt sich? Lies die Wörter und nummeriere das Reimwort.

1. blue **2.** hair **3.** map **4.** red **5.** look **6.** ten

[ ] 
[1] 
[ ] 
[2] 
[ ] 
[ ] 

2 Welche Wörter reimen sich? Nummeriere und vergleiche danach mit einem Partnerkind.

1. black	[ ] eight	**5.** free	[7] clown	**9.** get	[ ] match
2. great	[ ] mice	**6.** long	[ ] day	**10.** catch	[ ] feet
3. nice	[1] Jack	**7.** brown	[ ] strong	**11.** eat	[ ] book
4. toys	[ ] boys	**8.** play	[ ] tree	**12.** look	[ ] pet

3 Sprich dir die Wörter vor. Markiere das Wort, das nicht passt.

1. ○  ○  ○ 

2. ○  ○  ○ 

4 Fällt dir bei den Reimwörtern etwas auf? Denk einmal nach.

Wie hören sie sich an – wie werden sie geschrieben?
Werden alle Wörter, die sich gleich anhören auch gleich geschrieben?

Typically British?

1 Höre dir die Texte an und lies mit.

2 Höre dir die Texte noch einmal an und nummeriere die passenden Bilder.

1 In Britain you can see a lot of coffee shops but most people drink tea. They like their tea with sugar and milk. But in Turkey and Ireland even more people drink tea.

2 When you turn 5 you have to start school in Britain. On the first school day British children wear their new school uniform. They don't get a *Schultüte* filled with sweets or little presents like children in Germany.

3 In Great Britain you have to drive on the left. There are only four countries in Europe where people drive on the left, too. That can be difficult with a German car. When you want to cross the road, first look right and then left!

4 Traditional British food is simple but tastes good. You can find British food like fish and chips and sandwiches all over the world.

☐ 

☐ 

☐ 

☐ 

3 Finde den richtigen Titel für die Texte.

☐ Der britischer Verkehr ist gefährlich

☐ Viele Briten trinken immer noch gerne Tee

☐ Britische Kinder sind sehr jung, wenn sie in die Schule kommen

☐ Britisches Essen schmeckt nicht

CD 92

How to read

1 Schau dir die Überschift und das Bild an.

Ava's email

2 Lies die E-Mail. Unterstreiche die Wörter, die du nicht kennst.

Hi, my name is Ava Wilson. I would like to have a pen pal.

I will be 10 years old in September. I live in Manchester.

My family (that's my father, my mother, my brother Ron and me) lives in a big house with a garden. We've got a cat (Monster) and a rabbit (Luke). Every morning I feed our pets.

My school is near the church. I go to school by bike. My favourite subjects are Maths and German.

Every Saturday I go swimming with my dad. In summer we often go to the beach.

What about you? Would you like to be my pen pal?

I'm waiting for your answer,

Ava

Send

3 Um was geht es in der E-Mail?

○ Ava writes about her birthday party.

○ Ava writes about herself to find a pen pal.

4 Lies die E-Mail noch einmal. Erinnere dich an die vier Fragewörter. Vervollständige die Tabelle mit den Informationen über das Mädchen.

who = wer | where = wo | when = wann | what = was

Who, who, who – wer bist du?

Where, where, where – wo kommst du her?

who	
who she is:	Ava Wilson
who belongs to her family:	father, mother, brother
where	
where she lives:	Manchester
where they go in summer:	
when	
when she goes swimming:	every Saturday
when they go to the beach:	
what	
what she would like to have:	a pen pal
what her pets are:	
what her favourite subjects are:	

My words

countries

Canada .... 

Ireland .... 

the USA .... 

South Africa .... 

England, Great Britain  

Australia .... 

India .... 

____

at school

Maths ...... 

English .... 

Science .... 

German .... 

Music .... 

ICT .... 

PE .... 

Crafts ...... 

Art .... 

Assembly .. 

school dinner .. 

Golden time .... 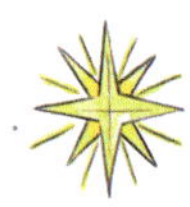

break .... 

timetable .... 

____

my day

get up .... 

get dressed .... 

brush my teeth ..... 

wash my face .... 

have breakfast .... 

go to school .... 

have lunch .... 

do my homework .... 

meet my friends .... 

watch TV .... 

have dinner .... 

take a shower .... 

put on my pyjamas .... 

go to bed .... 

in the morning .... 

in the afternoon .... 

in the evening .... 

____

time

o'clock

quarter past

half past

quarter to

places in town

police station

fire station

post office

town hall

hospital

cinema

fish and chip shop

market square

playground

graveyard

toy museum

church

park

directions

zebra crossing

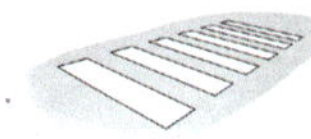

go straight on

turn left

turn right

cross

at the open day

talk to a police officer

sit in a police car

meet the police dogs

see the old toys

play old games

buy a souvenir

see the coloured glass windows

climb the tower

ring the bells

at the fish and chip shop

fish supper
single fish
sausage
chips
onion rings

crisps
salt
vinegar
water
lemonade

apple juice
orange juice
small
medium
large

jobs

builder
firefighter
shop assistant
police officer
nurse
bus driver

car mechanic
engineer
zookeeper
dentist
gardener
IT specialist

hairdresser
office worker
farmer
teacher
waiter
waitress

what people do at work

help ill or old people
sell things
check people's teeth
look after animals
help ill animals
cut hair

build bridges
work with computers
build houses
plant trees and flowers
repair cars

animals

horse . . . .

goat . . . .

pig . . . .

chicken . . . .

cow . . . . . .

turkey . . . .

snake . . . .

polar bear . . . .

rhino . . . .

tiger . . . .

parrot . . . .

penguin . . . .

chimpanzee . . .

crocodile . . . .

monkey . . . . . .

seal . . . .

kangaroo . .

hippo . . . .

camel . . . . .

panda . . . .

lion . . . .

llama . . . .

____

____

where animals come from

North America . .

South America . . . .

Europe . . . .

Africa . . . .

Asia . . . .

Australia . .

the Arctic . . .

the Antarctic . . . .

____

helping nature

go by bike . . .

take public transport . . . .

walk . . . .

switch on . . . .

switch off . . . .

save water . . .

save energy . . . . .

save petrol . . . .

collect rubbish . . .

buy second hand

repair things . . . .

recycle paper . . . .

newspapers

cans . . . .

batteries . . . .

broken glass . .

empty bottles . . . .

plastic wrappings .

Don't waste food! . . . .

____

water usage

- cooking
- body care
- flushing the toilet
- taking a shower
- watering the garden
- cleaning
- washing clothes
- washing the dishes

holidays

- sunglasses
- goggles
- sea
- air mattress
- flippers
- lifeguard
- campsite
- caravan
- seagull
- spade
- sun hat
- sun cream
- snorkel
- fishing net
- have a barbecue
- have a campfire
- lie in the sun
- build a sandcastle
- collect shells
- play beach volleyball
- go fishing
- go snorkelling
- go stand-up paddling
- go slacklining
- go swimming
- go climbing
- go biking

Thanksgiving

- pilgrims
- America
- ship
- Native Americans
- corn
- turkey
- parade

St Patrick's Day

- leprechaun
- pot of gold
- shamrock